Be Inspired by ME

"and all of me"

by

Olamidotun Votu-Obada

Illustrated by

Arooba Bilal

Shine your light xx

OVO

Feb 2024

"The greatest story ever written, is the one you will write about yourself"

Olamidotun Votu-Obada

This book belongs to:

____

"A one-of-a-kind, unique and special person".

Proudly Me forever!

Published in Canada.

Library Cataloguing-in-Publication Data is available

Paperback
ISBN 978-1-7782222-2-1

Find more information about the author at www.olamidotunvo.com

First Edition - Published in June 2022

Inspire HQ
www.myinspirebooks.com

Dedication

To my daughters Beulah, Hephzibah, and Jedidah
who inspire me to confidently be me every day!

And to every child around the world,
Inspire on, be You and be different!

Shine on and on.

O.V.O

I am me!

I can be anything I want to be and more.

Everyone is amazing in their own way.

I am not just another face in the crowd.

I am me.

Special me!

One-of-a-kind me!

Extraordinary me!

My gifts, talents and abilities know no bounds.
I am my own inspiration.

I am me!

I am the **first and only one of my kind.**
My gifts are unique to **Me**.

No other person can ever be
or live my life for me.
I am the only me.

Almost eight billion faces around the world,
And there will never be another me.

No one else will ever have the same combination of talent, ability, birth story, upbringing, tone of voice, colour of eyes and skin that make me.

I am original.
Oh so unique.
I am me.

I am beautiful. You **must** take a second look.
I am perfect. Wonderfully and excellently made.
I am one of a kind.

I am me!

I may have one talent, or I may have more.
I may be rich, or I may be poor.
I may be brown, peach, white, black or in between.

I may have two eyes, one or none.
I may have two ears, one or none.
I may have all my limbs, some, one, or none.
I may look different to the world.
None of these things change who I am.

I am me!

I do not wish to be anyone else.
Wonderful, special me.
I inspire Me to be more.
To be all I was meant to be!

I am Me.

I was born to impact the world around me.
The world will read about Me one day.
My story will be told for all to hear, see, and learn.

Some parts will be unimaginable.
Some parts will inspire.
Some parts will break records.
Some parts will give lasting impressions.
My story will be one worth retelling.
Most importantly, all parts will be about me!
All parts will be particular to just me.

I live with my purpose in mind.
I AM ME.

If I want to do anything, I put my mind to it. I work at it. I can do it.

I can do it!

I can do it!

I can do it!

I can do it!

I can dream.
Dreams are free.
And everything is achievable to me.

I may face challenges,
But it doesn't change who I was made to be!
I can overcome all things.
It's only a matter of time.
I will make it possible.

I am me!

Special me.
One-of-a-kind me.

I change the world by being uniquely me.
I change the world with the aura I bring.
I change the world with the smile on my face.
I change the world by being different.
I change the world by using my gifts and talents to help others.
I change the world with everything I am.

I am Me.

I am the greatest of all time
because

I am Me.

I am not an accident.
I am not a mistake.
I am more than my failures.
I am more than my mistakes.
I evolve, learn and grow daily.

One-of-a-kind Me.

The me I see in the mirror is going places!
I am amazingly and remarkably made.

Beautiful inside and out!

I am Me.

AND I LOVE ME!

I AM ME

Manufactured by Amazon.ca
Bolton, ON

37807388R00024